Book 2

The Baroque Spirit
1600–1750

Selected, edited and annotated by Nancy Bachus

21 Intermediate to Early Advanced Piano Solos
Reflecting the Influence of 16 Great Composers on the Baroque Period

Foreword

To understand and interpret musical style, one must recapture the spirit of the era in which composers lived, created and performed, and be aware of events that influenced them. During the 17th to mid-18th centuries, many forms and instruments that are part of modern concert life were new or in their infancy. The Baroque period marked the birth of opera and oratorio, and firmly established instrumental music as instruments improved and idiomatic writing developed. Many Baroque forms reached their height around 1750 in works of George Frideric Handel and Johann Sebastian Bach.

Although Bartolomeo Cristofori invented a keyboard instrument with a hammer mechanism around 1700, the piano was not in widespread use until the 1770s when it superseded the harpsichord. Since most Baroque keyboard music was written for and performed on an organ or harpsichord, Baroque composers seldom indicated performance instructions. As the music in this book will probably be played on a modern piano by students, the editor has added appropriate dynamics as well as slurs, staccato marks, rolled chords, tempo indications and ornament realizations.

1720–1770 Late Baroque and Rococo Styles—Transition to the Classical Period

The death of J. S. Bach in 1750 commonly marks the end of the Baroque and the beginning of the Classical period in music. The contrapuntal fugues of J. S. Bach and the piano sonatas of Franz Joseph Haydn and Wolfgang Amadeus Mozart illustrate great stylistic differences in only about a 30-year time span. The keyboard sonatas of Domenico Scarlatti and other events of the late-Baroque period laid the groundwork for them.

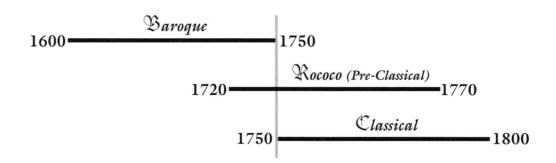

- The 1740s produced such great contrapuntal works as J. S. Bach's second set of preludes and fugues, The *Well-Tempered Clavier, Volume 2,* and Handel's *Messiah.*

- In France during the 1720s, the *style galant* (gallant style) emphasized melody and accompanying chords in music whose purpose was merely "to entertain."

- The major/minor tonal system and basics of modern harmony were recognized, laying the foundation for clear modulations to closely related keys.

- Music was performed more informally in salons, and public concerts began.

- Music publishing became more common to meet the demand for music by amateurs and self-taught musicians.

- Multi-movement suites, the pairing of Scarlatti's keyboard sonatas, and his use of two themes in a single movement show the seeds of Classical sonata form.

Contents

"Surely no one has ever questioned the need for ornaments...they enliven them [notes]; they give them a special, expressive quality and weight, where necessary...They help to explain their intention."

Carl Philipp Emanuel Bach[1]

Baroque Ornamentation

- Ornamentation was a vital part of Baroque music. Soloists were expected to "improve" their part with spontaneously improvised ornaments, and improvising was a prized skill. Like decorations, ornaments are *"not necessary to the structure ...but make it more pleasing."*[2]

- Notated ornaments were usually abbreviated with special signs, which could be interpreted by the performer with personal taste and freedom according to context.

Keyboard Ornamentation: Notated ornaments had symbols that varied by country.

- **Italian** composers seldom notated ornaments, expecting performers to improvise them, while **English** composers used a unique set of symbols.

- Seventeenth-century **French** lute composers' profuse ornamentation was carried over to harpsichord music, and the execution was specified in their manuscripts.

- French symbols were imported and adapted by many **German** composers. Carl Philipp Emanuel Bach (1714–1788), organized and clarified these into rules that were accepted until the time of Ludwig van Beethoven (1770–1827).

The following chart shows the accepted execution for frequently used Baroque ornaments; however, any of these realizations could vary within a specific musical context. Speed of execution depends upon the rhythm, tempo and character of the music.

Common Baroque Ornaments (German Symbols)

	Symbol	Beginning Note	Number of Notes	Direction	Rhythmic Beginning	Execution
Mordent	⌁	written note	3	down	on the beat	
Trill	⌁ or *tr*	note above	4 or more depending on the length of the ornamented note	down	on the beat	
Schneller (see page 10)	⌁ or *tr*	written note	3	up	on the beat	
Pralltriller		note above, but it's tied	same as trill	down	instantly after the beat (tie)	
Turn	∾	note above	4	down, then back up	where placed	

Long Appoggiatura: (leaning note) is played on the beat, thus delaying the principal note by half its length. If the principal note is a dotted note, the appoggiatura takes two thirds of its length.

With ordinary and dotted notes:

With a chord:

Short Appoggiatura: occurs most commonly before fast moving notes. It can be executed as a "crush," played on the beat, almost simultaneously with the principal note.

The editor suggests first learning the music in this collection without ornamentation, and then adding as many indicated ornaments as possible without interrupting the rhythmic flow or musical content.

[1]Alan Kendall, *The Chronicle of Classical Music* (London: Thames and Hudson, 1994), 97.

[2]Jean Rousseau in 1687, quoted in Edith Borroff's *Music in Europe and the United States* (Englewood Cliffs, NJ: Prentice-Hall, Inc., 1971), 292.

François Couperin (1668–1733)

*"Being **galant**, in general, means seeking to please."*
Voltaire (1694–1778), French author, philosopher[3]

François Couperin ("the Grand") was a composer at the Court of Louis XIV (1638–1715). The Couperin family was second in importance only to the Bach family dynasty. Couperin's **27 suites** (French *ordres*) of harpsichord music are considered to be his greatest works. These elegant, graceful pieces are fine examples of **rococo** and **style galant.** They *"charm, and perhaps move, but without tears of violent passions."* [4]

Style Galant (Gallant Style)

Toward the end of King Louis XIV's reign, many members of the Court were spending less time at Versailles and more in Paris and at their country homes entertaining in their own personal style. Upon Louis' death his young successor closed the Palace of Versailles and made his primary residence in Paris. As the arts moved from palaces into elegant salons, style galant and the rococo styles emerged.

- **Rococo** was apparently a combination of *baroco* (Italian for baroque) and *rocaille* (shellwork). Shell-like, curved designs were used in architecture and interior decoration in France and spread to other countries. *Rococo* was a delicate, more subtle **variation of the Baroque.**

- The word **galant**, widely used in 18th-century literature, painting and music, implied elegance, charm, grace, clarity, intimacy and naturalness in contrast to the dignified seriousness and impressive grandeur of **Baroque style.**

- The freer **style galant** in music had a lighter texture and emphasized melody (at times elaborately ornamented), supported by chords in a **homophonic texture.** The 18th-century music historian, Charles Burney, said *"...[the style galant called] attention...chiefly to the voice-part, by disentangling it from fugue, complication and laboured [sic] contrivance."*[5]

François Couperin's *The Art of Playing the Harpsichord* (1716) comments on harpsichord teaching and performing, including instructions for fingering and execution of ornaments. Since "good taste" was of great concern in French music, art, and life in general at this time, this treatise even directs how to please the audience by wearing a light smile while sitting at a harpsichord.

---

[3] *New Grove Dictionary of Music and Musicians*, s.v. "Galant" by Daniel Heartz (London: Macmillan, 1980), Vol. 7, 92.
[4] Paul Henry Lang and Otto Bettman, *A Pictorial History of Music* (New York: W. W. Norton & Co., 1960), 59.
[5] *New Grove's Dictionary*, "Galant," 93.

Suites (*ordres*)

- A **suite** is a set of pieces, usually dance-like and in the same key.

- Couperin's **suites** contain as many as 20 pieces in the same or closely related keys, which, unlike most suites, are not intended to be performed as a unit.

This title page published in 18th-century Paris illustrates the shell-like, curved designs so popular at this time

- These *ordres* are Couperin's personal version of the keyboard suite. Some were dance movements, but most were **descriptive pieces** with **fanciful titles** such as *The Butterflies*, *The Ticking Clock* and *The Nightingale in Love*.

- Rather than express his personal emotions, Couperin described what he saw. Some pieces contained hidden jokes while others were "character" portrayals of his family, his colleagues, members of the Court and even the King. They marked a new direction in music—moving away from serious music toward music intended for entertainment.

- This piece is from a set called *The Pageant of the Great and Ancient Musician's Guild*. The complete title is *Third Act: The Jugglers, Dancers, Tumblers: with Bears and Monkeys.*

Third Act: The Jugglers, Dancers

ⓐ Although Couperin requested all ornaments be played in his music, the editor suggests students learn this piece without ornaments, then add as many ornaments as possible without interrupting the rhythmic flow.

This piece is from a set titled *Les Dominos ou les Folies française* (The Dominos, or the French Follies). A **domino** was a large cape-like garment worn over costumes on the way to a masked ball. Each piece in the set is a satirical character study with such titles as *Modesty (under a pink domino)* and *Frenzy or Despair (under a black domino).*

A lady wearing a domino to a masked ball

The Flirt (under different dominos)

François Couperin
(1668-1733)

ⓐ Keep the eighth note steady throughout the changing meters.

"After Lully (1632–1687), all other musicians simply imitated him until Rameau came, when, by the depth of his harmony, he surpassed them and made of music a new art."

Voltaire (1694–1778)[6]

Jean-Philippe Rameau (1683–1764)

The harpsichord music of French composer Jean-Philippe Rameau is identified as **galant** or **rococo** in style. Royal Composer to King Louis XV, in his day Rameau was famous as an opera composer, a performer on organ and harpsichord, and was widely known as a philosopher and musical theorist.

Establishment of the major/minor tonal system

In his *Treatise on Harmony* (1722), Rameau made observations about the way composers were writing, and his insights and discoveries are still accepted as the basis for music theory.

- From the earliest harmonic music, composers, theorists and students of Western style music based harmonies on the relationship between intervals. Even in *basso continuo* (figured bass) harmony was identified by the intervals above the bass note.

- Rameau believed that all music is founded on harmony derived from natural principles of mathematics and the laws of acoustics. Instead of seeing separate intervals above a bass note, Rameau viewed the notes as a unit, what we call a **triad** (a chord built in thirds with a **root**), and he also wrote about its **inversions.** He identified the way chord progressions function, naming **tonic** and **dominant** harmonies, thus making **modulation** understandable.

- His theoretical studies and writings were vital in the development of harmonic thinking in Western music. He continued these studies until his death.

Rameau's Keyboard Music

Rameau wrote more than 65 keyboard pieces, which were published in four books during his lifetime. Most were dances or imitative pieces with descriptive titles like *Clouds of Dust Stirred up by Gusts of Wind, The Simpletons of Sologne,* or *The Hen.* Rameau used such varied techniques as chromatic dissonance and unusual modulations, and expressed greater emotional depth and virtuosity than previous keyboard writers.

[6]Derek Watson, ed. introduction and selection, *Dictionary of Musical Quotations* (Ware Hertfordshire: Cumberland House, Wordsworth Editions Ltd., 1994), 163.

The **menuet** was introduced by Jean-Baptiste Lully (1632–1687) to the Court of Louis XIV around 1650. Known as "the queen of dances," it became the most popular social dance of aristocratic society. This elegant dance had extremely small steps with a complex two-measure foot pattern, making an accent fall every six beats. The dance was usually performed by one couple at a time (after bowing to the King, or whomever was presiding) while others observed. The menuet has been described as a ritualistic courtship and inspired composers to write thousands of pieces in its form.

Menuet at a formal Court Ball

Menuet in G Minor

Jean-Philippe Rameau
(1683–1764)

ⓐ The editor suggests playing a **Schneller** ("snap" or inverted mordent) in measures 7, 8, 15 and 16. This ornament **begins on the main note, on the beat** and was used in the Baroque period on fast moving notes when there was no time for a complete trill. It was also used to avoid striking consecutive notes, such as in a descending line. The Schneller should not be overused.

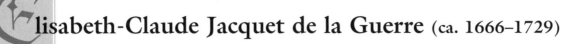Elisabeth-Claude Jacquet de la Guerre (ca. 1666–1729)

For four years a wonder has appeared here [Paris]. She [Elisabeth Jacquet] sings at sight the most difficult music. She accompanies herself, and others who wish to sing, at the harpsichord, which she plays in an inimitable manner. She composes pieces and plays them in all the keys asked of her, … and she still is only ten years old.

Mercure galant (French newspaper), 1677[7]

The **Jacquet family** was known as musicians and instrument builders. Elisabeth's father, Claude Jacquet(II) (n.d.–1702), was an organist and harpsichordist, and her grandfathers were outstanding harpsichord makers. Elisabeth is considered to be the greatest of this musical lineage.

- She appeared at the Court of Louis XIV who was so impressed with her talent that she was invited to live at Versailles where she was educated for several years. The King attended her performances and allowed her to dedicate compositions to him.

- Later, she married organist, Marin de la Guerre. They lived in Paris and she composed and performed in private homes and public theaters where, *"all the great musicians and fine connoisseurs went eagerly to hear her."*[8]

- Her compositions include harpsichord pieces, chamber music, songs, cantatas, a ballet and an opera, performed at the Royal Academy of Music in Paris. Many of these works were also published during her lifetime. Her *Te Deum* was performed in the Chapel of the Louvre to honor Louis XV's recovery from smallpox.

- A 1678 issue of the *Mercure galant* declared her to be *"the marvel of our century."*[9] A commemorative medal with her portrait was issued shortly after her death and bore the inscription, *"With the great musicians I competed for the prize."*

- This *Rigaudon* (a dance) is from la Guerre's second book of harpsichord pieces, published in 1707. The title for the collection suggests they may be performed with violin accompaniment. In concerts at this time, violinists sometimes doubled the treble line, playing softly so as not to detract from the harpsichord part.

Rigaudon

Elisabeth-Claude Jacquet de la Guerre
(ca. 1666–1729)

[7]Carol Neuls-Bates, ed., *Women in Music* (New York: Harper & Row, 1982), 62.
[8]*New Grove Dictionary*, "Jacquet de la Guerre, Elisabeth-Claude," 455.
[9]Ibid., 455.

Jean Baptiste Loeillet (1680–1730)

Born in Belgium, **Loeillet** (also known as John Loeillet) settled in London about 1705 where he became a famous and prosperous harpsichord teacher and performer. He wrote several books of harpsichord pieces that were published during his lifetime. Loeillet also played flute and oboe in various orchestras and is credited with introducing the transverse flute to England. There it became fashionable and replaced the recorder.

Since the English pronounced his last name as "Lully," at first the London public believed him to be the Frenchman, Jean-Baptiste Lully (1632–1687) from Louis XIV's Court. This piece, composed by Jean Baptiste Loeillet, is attributed to Jean-Baptiste Lully in many collections even today.

Aire is a term used for a tune, song or melody. In sets of harpsichord pieces, it referred to a piece more melodic than dance-like in character.

Aire

Jean Baptiste Loeillet
(1680–1730)

George Frideric Handel (1685–1759)

Although born in Germany, **Handel's** travels made him an international composer. His original style was a blend, showing Italian influence in his operas and oratorios, and Italian, German and French traits in his harpsichord pieces.

■ Handel's success with Italian opera led him to London. There he received an annual pension from Queen Anne (1665–1714), and later from King George I of England (1660–1727), while also producing and promoting his operas and oratorios for the new concert-going public.

■ His organ improvisations and performances during the intermissions of his oratorios made him a well-known personality, popular with London nobility and commoners.

■ Handel's keyboard music, some written for the royal princesses, was first published in 1720. The pieces emphasized melody with harmonic support rather than strict polyphonic lines, and the rapid scales and broken chord patterns illustrate his **idiomatic keyboard writing.**

■ Blind the last seven years of his life, he continued to compose, perform at the organ and conduct oratorio performances. His works are published in 100 volumes.

Title page of the first edition (1720)

*Portrait of Handel
by T. Hudson*

[10]Watson, *Dictionary of Musical Quotations*, 149.

Although common with French composers, this **descriptive title**, given by Handel, is the only one found in his keyboard pieces. "Impertinent" means irrelevant, of no value, a title similar to Couperin's *Le Petit-Rien* (The Little Nothing). Rudeness (not showing proper respect) is another meaning for impertinence. In the opening, the left hand enters in **imitation**, interrupting the right hand before it has finished stating the motive.

Impertinence

George Frideric Handel
(1685–1759)

ⓐ The editor suggests playing the half notes slightly detached.

Throughout this period dancing was popular in aristocratic ballrooms, and multitudes of dances were published for harpsichord. Originally a folk dance, the gavotte was introduced to the Court of Louis XIV and became a regular part of formal court balls. The phrases are generally four bars long with a rhythmic point of arrival in the fourth measure.

Gavotte in G Major

George Frideric Handel
(1685–1759)

The First Public Concerts

Public concerts, given by amateurs as well as professional musicians, began in England in the late-17th century. They were held in taverns, theaters, assembly rooms and newly built concert halls.

Concerts always included a variety of performers—groups of instrumentalists as well as vocal soloists and keyboard artists.

In the early-18th century, most concerts were held in theaters and **pleasure gardens**, the most famous being Vauxhall Gardens, originally a manor house and grounds. In spring and summer, tree-lined walks, refreshment booths, and entertainment were enjoyed for a small fee. All classes of people flocked there, and *Vauxhall Songs* were published for more than a century.

Vauxhall Gardens, where Handel's music was frequently performed and his Royal Fireworks *music was first rehearsed*

Photos: Image Select/Art Resource, NY

Sonatas

The term **sonata** literally means a "sounded" piece, referring originally to any instrumental piece, and ultimately to one having two to four movements. During the 18th century it was used to describe both the **binary sonatas** of Domenico Scarlatti (1685–1757) and Handel, and the **multi-movement sonatas** of composers like Baldassare Galuppi (1706–1785) and Thomas Arne (1710–1778).

Handel opens the following two-part **binary sonata** with the principal motive in the tonic key of A major, then it **modulates** (changes key) to the dominant (E major) at the beginning of the **B** section (pickup to measure 11). The principal motive is restated yet again in the tonic when it returns to the home key of A major at the pickup to measure 21.

Sections: **A**   :‖: **B**   :‖

Key relationships: I   V :‖: V I :‖

Sonata in A Major

SECTION A
Allegretto

George Frideric Handel
(1685–1759)

ⓐ The notes in parentheses in measures 1, 3, 13 and 21 are played by the left hand.

Key: A Major

Henry Purcell (1659–1695)

Henry Purcell was one of the greatest composers of the Baroque period as well as one of the best English composers of all time. He enjoyed fame and prestige during his lifetime.

- Purcell's childhood was spent as a choir boy in the Chapel Royal, and one of his three-voice songs was published when he was eight years old. At age 15 he was hired at Westminster Abbey to keep the organ in tune and to copy organ music. He became the organist a few years later.

- Later appointed singer and organist for the Chapel Royal, he eventually became the keeper of the King's instruments, seeing that they were cleaned, repaired and tuned. He held this position for three different monarchs and composed music for all of them.

- His compositions include sacred music, theater music, vocal songs and instrumental works, with his most famous work being an opera, *Dido and Aeneas*.

- His keyboard works are only a small part of his total ouput and include eight **suites** or **lessons**. Most have an **almand, corant** and **saraband** (Purcell's spelling), standard for suites of the time, but each begins with a **prelude,** which is unusual.

Aeneas Telling Dido of the
Misfortunes of Troy (*1815*)
by P. N. Guérin

Knights of the Bath at Westminster Abbey *(1749) by Caneletto*

Purcell was organist at Westminster Abbey for 18 years.
Both he and Handel are buried there.

© Dean and Chapter of Westminster, London

This piece exhibits dance-like characteristics and demonstrates
Purcell's outstanding ability to write beautiful melodies.

Lilliburlero. A New Irish Tune

Henry Purcell (1659–1695)
Z. 646

Carl Philipp Emanuel Bach (1714–1788)

C.P.E. Bach was the second surviving and most famous son of Johann Sebastian Bach (1685–1750). He wrote five short pieces, which are found in the *Notebook for Anna Magdalena Bach*.

Notebook for Anna Magdalena Bach

Even though printed music existed in Germany in the early-18th century, it was not easy to secure, and true music lovers copied their favorite pieces. In 1725 Johann Sebastian Bach presented a beautiful book as a birthday gift to his second wife, Anna Magdalena Bach, that would be used for family music making. Some of the pieces were composed and copied by him into the book, some are in Anna's hand, some are by the children, and other pieces are by well-known composers of the day. The music included family favorites and was used for keyboard instruction, for instruction in composition, for Anna (a professional vocalist) to sing, for the children's dancing lessons, and for other special occasions.

The **polonaise,** a stately dance in triple meter, originated in court ceremonies and processions in 16th-century Poland. Characteristic are rhythmic divisions of the first beat; feminine phrase endings (ending on beat 2 or 3); and short, precise motives that are repeated.

Polonaise in G Minor

Carl Philipp Emanuel Bach (1714–1788)
BWV Anhang 125

---

[12]Ian Crofton and Donald Fraser, *A Dictionary of Musical Quotations* (New York: Schirmer Books, 1985), 11.

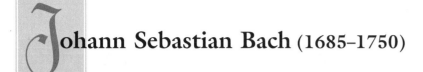ohann Sebastian Bach (1685–1750)

J. S. Bach did not live in a large cosmopolitan city or travel extensively. His entire life was spent in a region of Germany where he was known as an organ virtuoso and composer, a craftsman doing assigned tasks to the best of his ability. He took all styles, techniques and existing musical forms, except opera, and with his genius, brought them to perfection.

The Well-Tempered Clavier

Bach wrote two sets of **24 preludes and fugues,** *The Well-Tempered Clavier, Volumes I and II,* "*for the Use and Profit of young Musicians anxious to learn, and as a pastime for others already expert in the Art.*"[14] Each book has a prelude and fugue in the 12 major and minor keys, in ascending order. Lute frets mark **12 equal semitones in an octave,** but keyboard instruments were usually tuned with perfect intervals requiring re-tuning for some keys. With this cycle Bach endorsed equal-tempered tuning for keyboards and created works for teaching and pleasure.

Most of the preludes have one musical idea or technical pattern and are examples of different compositional forms. The fugues illustrate every possibility in fugal writing and techniques of **counterpoint** (interweaving melodic lines or voices), while also being a "*library of human emotion(s).*"[15] The *Well-Tempered Clavier, Volumes I and II* have been nicknamed the pianist's *Old Testament* with Beethoven's 32 Piano Sonatas the *New Testament.* To Robert Schumann (1810–1856) it was the "*musician's daily bread.*"[16]

Collegium Musicum

In the Baroque period various musical societies were active in German-speaking states. For seven years Bach directed the **Collegium Musicum,** which met at a coffee house in Leipzig and performed many of his chamber and orchestral works. The harpsichord concertos he wrote for them are the first solo keyboard concertos.

[13]Barbara Russano Hanning, *Concise History of Western Music* (New York: W. W. Norton, 1998), 264.
[14]Charles Sanford Terry, *The Music of Bach, An Introduction* (New York: Dover, 1963), 30.
[15]Ernest Hutcheson, *The Literature of the Piano* (New York: Alfred A. Knopf, 1952), 32.
[16]Patricia Fallows-Hammond, *Three Hundred Years at the Keyboard* (Berkeley, CA: Rose Books, 1984), 11.

Photo: AKG London

A performance of a collegium musicum at a coffee house

Bach wrote the **little preludes** as well as the **inventions** for alternatives to the finger exercises he gave his beginning students before they studied his "own greater compositions."[17]

Little Prelude in F Major

Johann Sebastian Bach (1685–1750)
BWV 927

ⓐ The editor suggests playing the left-hand eighth notes slightly detached.

[17]David Schulenberg, *The Keyboard Music of J.S. Bach* (New York: Schirmer, 1992), 151.

Originating in France, the **bourrée** was a quick duple-meter dance with an upbeat. During the reign of Louis XIV (1638–1715), the bourrée was fashionable as a social dance and appeared in theatrical ballets. In this **stylized harpsichord piece**, characteristics of the dance remain but it was never intended for dancing.

This **bourrée** is from the *Suite in E Minor for Lute*. It is believed that Bach played his lute works on the keyboard, and they were written in a traditional score rather than in lute tablature. One original manuscript of this suite has a notation that it was composed for lute-harpsichord (a harpsichord with gut strings imitating the sound of a lute). Bach owned two lute-harpsichords at the time of his death.

Bourrée in E Minor

Johann Sebastian Bach (1685–1750)
BWV 996

ⓐ The editor suggests playing the left-hand quarter notes slightly detached.

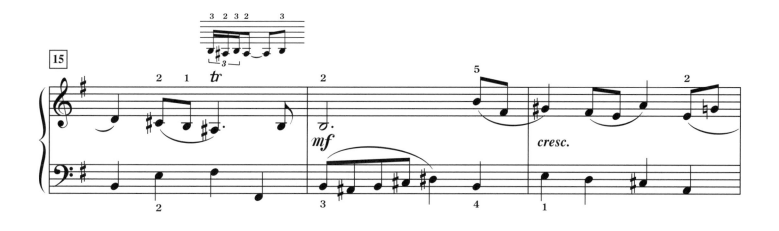

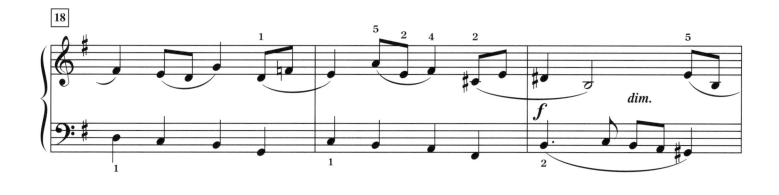

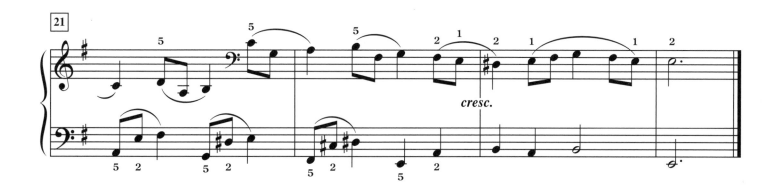

On J. S. Bach's appointment as Cantor at Leipzig, Graupner having refused:

"Since the best cannot be had, we must accept the mediocre."
Abraham Platz, Mayor of Leipzig (1723)[18]

Christoph (Johann) Graupner (1683–1760)

An outstanding keyboard performer and prolific composer, **Graupner** wrote 1418 church cantatas, 113 symphonies, about 50 concertos, 80 overtures, 36 sonatas, 5 operas, and a wide variety of keyboard music. A pupil and copyist for Johann Kuhnau (1660–1722), who was the Cantor for St. Thomas in Leipzig, Graupner applied to be his successor. The position was first offered to Georg Philipp Telemann (1681–1767) who withdrew, and then to Graupner. When his employer would not release him, the third choice, Johann Sebastian Bach, was appointed. An **intrada** is an instrumental piece used to announce or accompany an entrance, a special event, or to open a dance suite. Many are march-like in character.

Intrada

Christoph (Johann) Graupner
(1683–1760)

ⓐ The editor suggests playing the left-hand quarter notes slightly detached.

[18]Christopher Headington, *J. S. Bach* (New York: Simon & Schuster, 1994), 66.

Georg Philipp Telemann (1681–1767)

Telemann may have written more music than any composer in the history of music—over 3,000 works. During his lifetime he and Handel were considered to be the greatest living composers, and he had great influence on musical life throughout Germany.

- Unwilling to be limited by his contract as Cantor for the city of Hamburg, Telemann also wrote for the public opera house and organized concerts that enabled middle- class people to hear many different types of music.

- In many compositions he purposely avoided extreme technical difficulties, keeping the music accessible for amateurs and self-taught musicians. He also published, advertised and distributed his music, making printed music easily available for the first time.

Dances in Baroque Society

Court dances were present at all levels of society, and the elaborate choreography required practice to develop the skill necessary to secure and enhance social status. French court dances became the model, and **French dancing masters** (with their manuals) traveled throughout Europe.

- Dancing was considered to be healthful exercise for women, and was a necessary skill for men along with fencing and riding.

- Dancing lessons for children included instruction on how to sit, stand, bow and curtsy, and walk elegantly. There were numerous dancing schools and private tutors, and dance was part of the curriculum at many boarding schools.

The Dance Suite

Rhythmic patterns from dances pervaded all Baroque music, and instrumental pieces inspired by court dances were frequently grouped into **suites.** The dances differed in tempo, meter, character and national origin, but were in the same key. Between 1650 and 1750, most **keyboard dance suites** included an **allemande, courante, sarabande** and **gigue,** with **optional dances (bourrée, minuet, gavotte, polonaise)** placed before the gigue.

Venetian Woman and a Dancing Master
by Pietro Longhi (1702–1785)

[19]Crofton and Fraser, *Musical Quotations,* 136.

This suite is found in the *Little Keyboard Book for Wilhelm Friedemann Bach,* presented to him by his father, Johann Sebastian Bach, when he was nine years old. J. S. Bach was thought to have composed this suite, but research now names Telemann as the composer. It has only three movements (**allamande**, **corrente** and **gigue**), omitting the **sarabande**, usually found in the standard Baroque suite.

The **allemande** opened most suites.

- Originating in Germany, this duple-meter dance had a serious and dignified character and intricate footwork. In one part, dancers placed their hands on their hips and performed a series of little springing steps and sliding gallops.

- In the harpsichord form of the allemande, independent from dancing, the underlying harmony is the dominant feature. The **motivic imitation** between the hands and the running 16th notes of this allemande are typical of the form.

Suite in A Major

Allemande

Georg Philipp Telemann
(1681–1767)

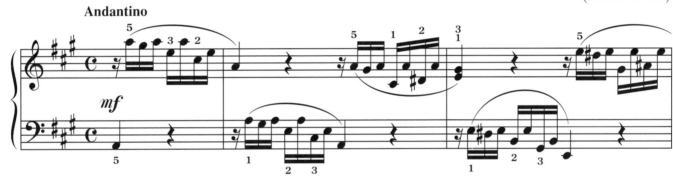

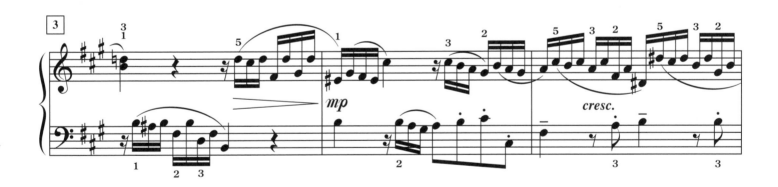

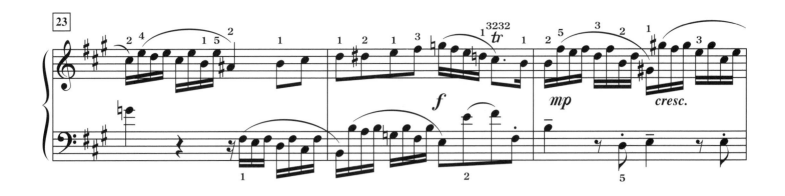

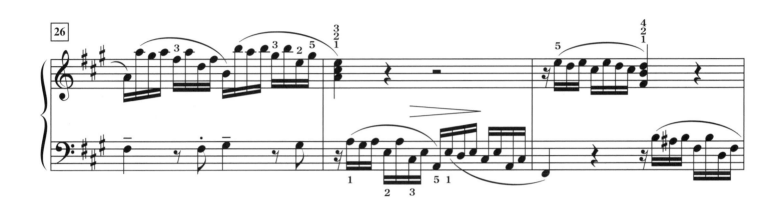

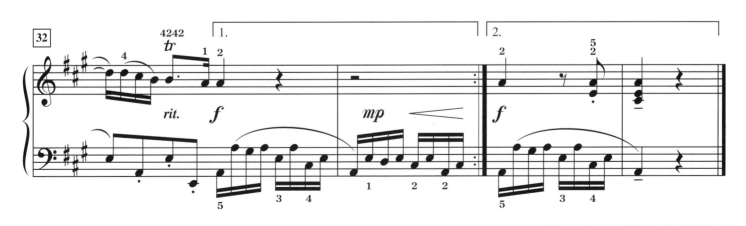

The **courante** (to run), originally a courtship dance, used mostly hop-step combinations. Popular in both France and Italy, different types developed in each country. The **French courante** is slower, more contrapuntal in style and usually in compound meter. This **corrente** is **Italian in style** with simple triple meter and running eighth notes. Frequent **imitation** at the beginning of phrases is typical of keyboard courantes.

An engraving by Duclos of an 18th-century ball

Corrente

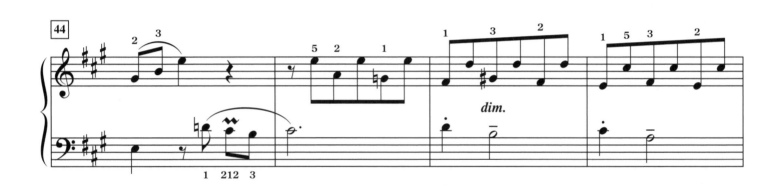

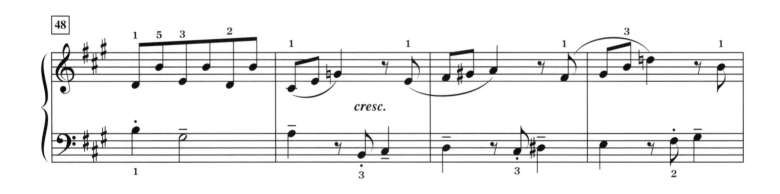

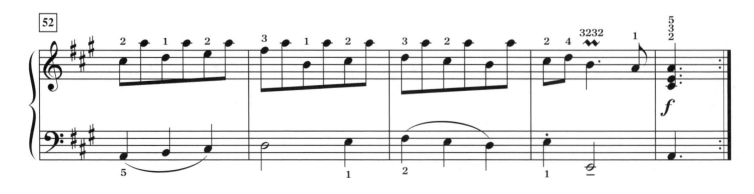

The **gigue** (to frolic or leap), was a lively, joyous dance with virtuoso footwork. Originating in England and Ireland, **"jigs" became "gigues"** in Lully's French ballets and were stylized for lute and harpsichord collections. Typically in compound triple meter with uneven rhythm (short-long, short-long) and **fugal or imitative texture**, it was the liveliest dance in a suite, bringing it to a brilliant conclusion.

A 17th-century French ballet dancer

Gigue

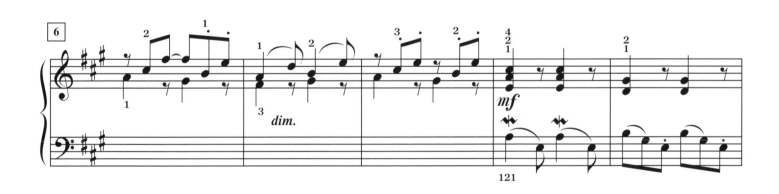

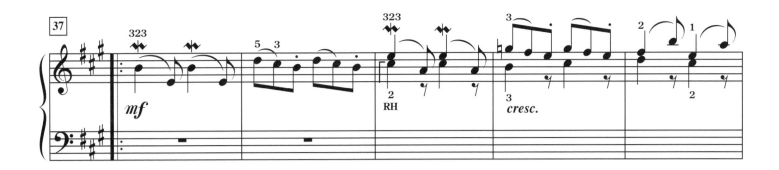

> *"He [Scarlatti] devoted himself to the harpsichord with an exclusiveness for which Chopin's cultivation of the piano offers the only parallel...he attained a technical elegance and virtuosity which also may be compared to Chopin."*
>
> Willi Apel (1893–1988), music scholar[20]

Domenico Scarlatti (1685–1757)

Believed by many to be the greatest harpsichord virtuoso of all time, **Domenico Scarlatti** developed a **true keyboard idiom** in his nearly 560 **binary sonatas**. One of the most original of all composers, his use of repeated notes (a guitar effect), rapid scales and double notes, crossing hands, wide leaps, arpeggios, and contrasts in register created a new level of technical brilliance for the instrument and paved the way for the piano literature.

Born in Naples, Scarlatti became Master of the Chapel at the Court in Lisbon, Portugal. One of his duties was to train the King's talented daughter, Maria Barbara (1711–1758), to play the harpsichord. When she married the heir to the Spanish throne, Scarlatti also went to Madrid and spent the rest of his life in Spain writing most of the sonatas there.

Essercizi per Cembalo (Exercises for Harpsichord)

Scarlatti's fame in his lifetime rested primarily on a set of 30 sonatas published in London and reprinted in other European cities.

The general title was *Essercizi* (exercises), but individual pieces were named *Sonatas*. It is thought that they were intended as a type of **etude** or study since each was based on a specific technical device or figuration.

Design on the title page of Essercizi per Cembalo *(1738)*

From the Preface:
...do not expect to find...any profound intention, but rather an ingenious gesting of the art, to prepare you for bold playing on the harpsichord...increase your own pleasure...

Curarum Levamen
(for the alleviation of boredom)

Scarlatti portrait by Gemälde von Antonio de Velasco

Scarlatti's Sonatas

- The sonatas are in **binary** (two-part) **form**, but are of infinite variety.

- It is believed they were intended to be performed in pairs or groups of three.

- **Imitation** is common, but there is no consistent contrapuntal writing.

- He frequently introduces a second theme at the point of modulation in the opening section.

- Scarlatti's modulations are firm but return to the home key in the second half, showing the seeds of Classical sonata form.

[20]Willi Apel, *Masters of the Keyboard* (Cambridge, MA: Harvard University Press, 1965), 164.

Sonata in D Minor

Gavotte

Domenico Scarlatti (1685–1757)
K. 64; L. 58

ⓐ At times Scarlatti used strong dissonant tones in his chords. He meant them to be harsh and startling so they should not be played timidly. If necessary, the left-hand major second (A, B) could be redistributed to the right hand.

theme 2

Key: D Minor

previous phrase
now slightly elaborated

Sonata in C Minor

Domenico Scarlatti (1685–1757)
K. 11; L. 352

SECTION A

Andante

theme 1 *mp*

Key: C Minor

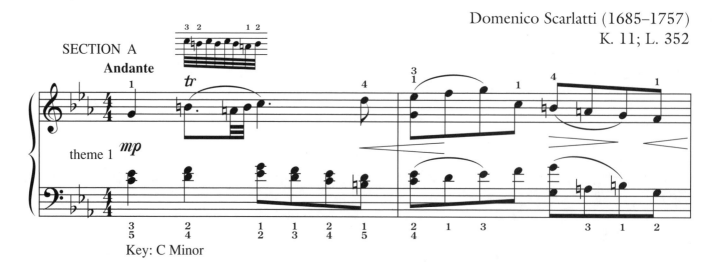

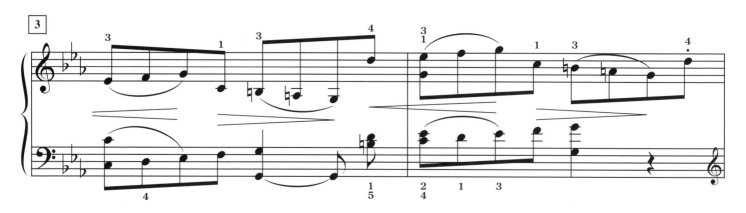

theme 2 in
modulating passage

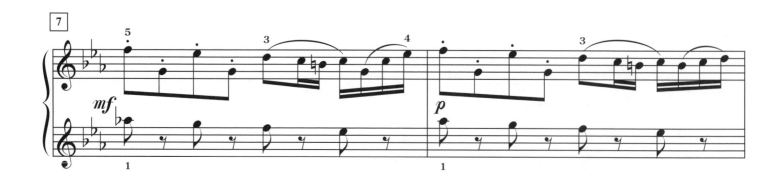

Key: G Minor

change from G Minor
to G Major

SECTION B

Key: G Major

theme 2 in modulating passage

theme 3 in C Minor

Key: C Minor

Domenico Zipoli (1688–1720)

An Italian organist and composer, **Zipoli** had keyboard pieces published in Rome and reprinted in London and Paris. He served as a Jesuit missionary to Argentina. Copies of his sacred music were found in several South American countries in the early 18th century.

Sarabande

Domenico Zipoli
(1688–1720)

Carlos de Seixas (1704–1742)

(sā-shus)

*Carlos Seixas,
engraving by
J. Daullé*

Carlos Seixas was a virtuoso keyboard performer and the leading Portuguese composer of the 18th century. Both he and Domenico Scarlatti were granted knighthoods by King John V (1689–1750) of Portugal in 1738.

■ At age 14 Seixas became the organist of Coimbra Cathedral and was appointed organist of the Royal Chapel two years later where Domenico Scarlatti was already employed. The two men were colleagues for nine years before Scarlatti left for the Spanish Court.

■ Seixas wrote over 700 keyboard **toccatas**, but only 88 survived after the 1755 Lisbon earthquake. His style is typical of keyboard **sonatas** of the transitional period from Baroque to Classical. Some have a single movement (Scarlatti's form) and others have three, four, or five movements.

During the Baroque period the term **toccata** (to touch) referred to different styles of music, at times free in form and multi-sectional. Almost all toccatas were written for a solo keyboard instrument, show idiomatic writing and display technical ability.

Toccata in C Minor

Carlos de Seixas
(1704–1742)

ⓐ The quarter notes should be slightly detached.   [21] *New Grove Dictionary,* "Seixas, Carlos de," 115.

...Those lesser thirds so plaintive, sixths diminished, sigh on sigh...
Oh, they praised you, I dare say! Brave Galuppi! that was music!
excerpt from Robert Browning's poem,
A Toccata of Galuppi's[22]

Baldassare Galuppi (1706–1785)

A popular Venetian opera composer, **Galuppi** spent time in London where his **keyboard sonatas** were first published. The sonatas are in various forms. Some are in single movement binary form like those of Scarlatti, while others show the budding of Classical sonata form with **several movements** related by key. At times his sonatas show a **change in texture** from **polyphonic** (several different melodic lines played simultaneously) to **homophonic** (a prominent melody accompanied by chordal harmony.) Galuppi's lyrical gift is evident in this elegant *Adagio,* the first of his four-movement *Sonata in D Major.*

Adagio

Baldassare Galuppi
(1706–1785)

[22]H. C. Robbins Landon and John Julius Norwisch, *Five Centuries of Music in Venice* (London: Thames and Hudson, 1991), 140.

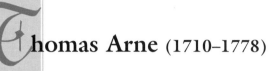

Thomas Arne (1710–1778)

An English composer, violinist, and organist, **Thomas Arne** was the leading composer of English theatrical music in the mid-18th century. He is best known today for his songs, including *The Lass with the Delicate Air* and *Rule, Britannia*.

- Arne's father was an upholsterer in Covent Garden who sent his son to be educated at Eton College, planning to apprentice him to an attorney. Arne developed his musical gifts by smuggling a **spinet** (small harpsichord) into his room, muffling the strings so he could practice unknown to his family. He also borrowed a uniform so he could be admitted to the servant's gallery of the Italian Opera in London.

- His father consented to musical studies and a career after hearing Thomas perform. He composed songs for Shakespeare's plays, wrote masques, oratorios, 30 operas, and held the position as composer for Vauxhall Gardens for many years. His greatest success came with the opera, *Artaxerxes,* the first Italian-style opera in English. It was produced regularly for over 70 years after its 1762 premiere.

Engraving of a riot at Covent Garden in 1763. Artarxerxes was so popular that when management withdrew cut-price tickets, it caused a riot.

- Most of Arne's works were lost in fires, but many were published in his lifetime, including annual collections of songs, overtures and a set of *Eight Sonatas or Lessons for Harpsichord* (two to four movements in each). It is known that Arne owned Scarlatti's *Essercizi* and influence is evident. When looking at all of Arne's works, his keyboard music is insignificant. Its value is in the quality of the music.

In the following two-movement sonata, Arne shows elements of **both the sonata and the suite**. The second movement is a **gigue**, the final movement of a dance suite, and the first movement is a **rounded binary form** but is moving closer to the classic **sonata-allegro** form. The second (**B**) section opens traditionally in the relative major (B-flat), then develops previous material, including the opening theme now in D minor. The **A** section is slightly elaborated when it returns.

[23] *New Grove Dictionary*, "Arne, Thomas," 608.

Sonata No. 6 in G Minor

Thomas Arne
(1710–1778)

SECTION A

Affettuoso
(With affection, tenderness)

theme 1 in G Minor

SECTION B

theme 1 in B♭ Major

theme 1 in D Minor

theme 1 returns
in G Minor

ⓐ The editor suggests playing the short appoggiatura as a "crush," on the beat almost simultaneously with the main note.

Coda (based on triplet patterns)

Gigue

Allegro

SECTION A

theme 1 in G Major

theme 2 in D Major

ⓐ The editor suggests playing the short appoggiaturas in measures 4, 34, 36, 38, 39 and 41 as a "crush," on the beat almost simultaneously with the main note.

SECTION B

theme 1 in D Major

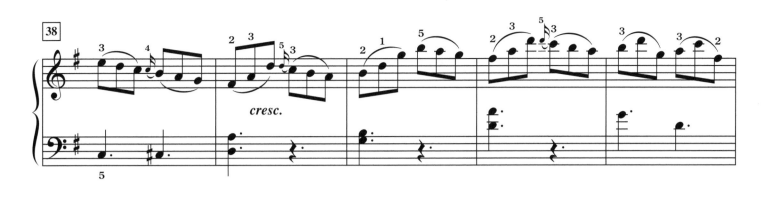

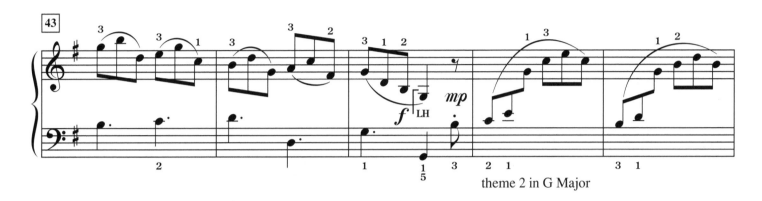

theme 2 in G Major

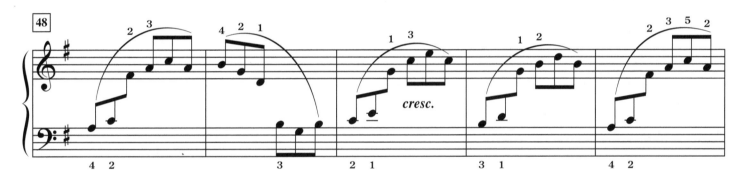

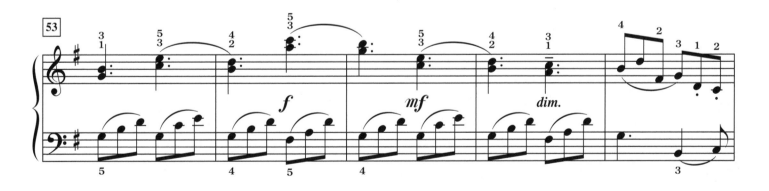

Padre Antonio Soler (1729–1783)

Perhaps the most gifted Spanish composer of the 18th century, **Soler** was known as an organist and for his treatise on modulation. A Catholic monk, he became the *maestro de capilla* of Escorial in Spain (a monastery and royal palace). During the reign of Ferdinand VI (1712–1759) and Maria Barbara (1711–1758), the royal family spent extended time there, and Soler studied with Domenico Scarlatti. Soler wrote at least **120 keyboard sonatas**, 27 of which were published in London in 1796. There was a **pianoforte** at Escorial, and some sonatas appear to have been written for it. Soler's sonatas exhibit use of **Spanish folk elements and guitar effects**.

Sonata in C Minor

Padre Antonio Soler
(1729–1783)

Andantino cantabile

[24]John Gillespie, *Five Centuries of Keyboard Music* (Belmont, CA: Wadsworth, 1965), 112.

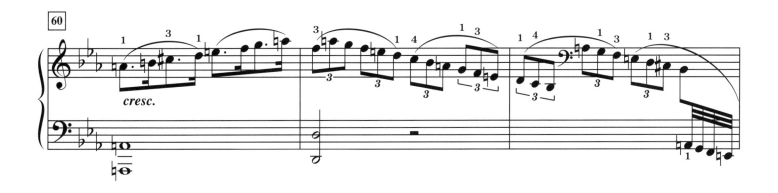